# HAZY SKIES

# HAZY SKIES

## WEATHER AND THE ENVIRONMENT

by Jonathan D. W. Kahl

Lerner Publications Company / Minneapolis

*For Sam and Joe*

All words printed in **bold** are explained in the
glossary that begins on page 60.
A metric conversion chart appears on page 64.

Website address: www.lernerbooks.com

Library of Congress Cataloging-in-Publication data

Kahl, Jonathan D.
    Hazy skies : weather and the environment / by Jonathan D.W. Kahl.
      p.   cm.
    Includes index.
    Summary: Describes the connections between pollution and weather,
  the destruction of the ozone layer, global warming, efforts at pollution
  control, and alternative energy forms.
    ISBN 0-8225-2530-5 (alk. paper)
    1. Weather — Environmental aspects — Juvenile literature. 2. Air —
  Pollution— Environmental aspects — Juvenile literature.
  [1. Weather. 2. Air — Pollution. 3. Pollution.] I. Title.
  QC981.3.K28 1998
  363.73'92 — dc20                                        96-42084

Manufactured in the United States of America
1 2 3 4 5 6 – JR – 03 02 01 00 99 98

# CONTENTS

INTRODUCTION / 6

**1** NOT A NEW PROBLEM / 10

**2** POLLUTED SKIES / 20

**3** NEGATIVE EFFECTS / 26

**4** THE ROLE OF WEATHER / 32

**5** OZONE DESTRUCTION / 44

**6** A WARMING TREND / 50

**7** THE NEXT STEP? / 56

GLOSSARY / 60

INDEX / 62

HOW'S THE WEATHER?

# INTRODUCTION

The **atmosphere,** the blanket of gas that surrounds the Earth, is kind of an international treasure. Nowhere else can you see thunderstorms, sunsets, rainbows, and clouds—all for free. The atmosphere also provides us with some necessities of life, such as the oxygen we breathe and the water we drink (which falls as rain and snow).

The atmosphere protects us too. The **ozone layer,** a section of the atmosphere about 15 miles above the ground, filters out harmful energy from the Sun. Higher up, the atmosphere protects us from meteors traveling through space. Millions of meteors—from tiny specks of dust to huge boulders—hurl through the outer atmosphere every day. Most meteors burn up when they hit the atmosphere. They disappear before they can hit the ground and cause damage.

The atmosphere is truly a remarkable provider, protector, and entertainer. Yet, because it surrounds us every minute of every day, most people don't think about it very often. Worse, people tend to take the atmosphere for granted—they even pollute it.

The atmosphere helps make life on Earth possible. It also entertains us with incredible shows of changing weather.

**Air pollution,** contamination of the atmosphere, can take many forms. Air pollution can be gas, such as carbon monoxide from car exhaust. It can be solid, such as tiny particles of soot from a factory smokestack. It can even be liquid, such as tiny droplets of acid that form when chemical reactions take place in the air. Air pollution in any form can harm human, animal, and plant life. Air pollution can even damage books and buildings.

Air pollution comes from many sources. Factories and power plants release tons of polluting gases and particles into the air each day. Household furnaces release carbon monoxide and other harmful gases. Cars, motorcycles, trucks, buses, boats, airplanes, and construction equipment release carbon monoxide, as well as poisonous minerals such as lead. Other air pollution comes from cigarette smoke, fireplaces, and forest

## LAYERS OF THE ATMOSPHERE

The atmosphere is divided into several different layers. The layer closest to the Earth's surface is called the troposphere. Most air pollution is found in this layer, where it may be moved about by the wind or returned to the Earth in rain and snow.

Above the troposphere we find the stratosphere, which includes the "ozone layer." The ozone layer protects us by filtering out harmful ultraviolet radiation from the Sun. Scientists have discovered that certain forms of air pollution, in combination with specific weather conditions, can lead to destruction of the protective ozone layer.

Above the stratosphere are the mesosphere and, finally, the thermosphere. There is no distinct upper boundary to the atmosphere—the air at the top of the thermosphere is so thin that it slowly blends into space.

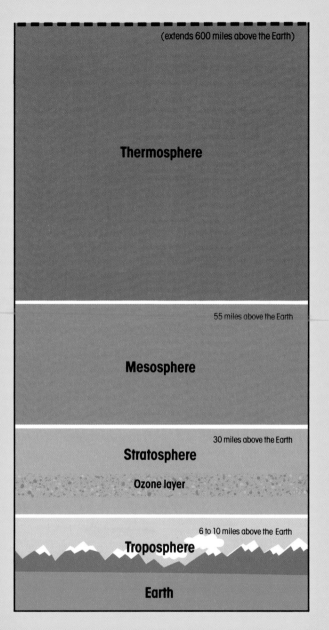

(extends 600 miles above the Earth)

**Thermosphere**

55 miles above the Earth

**Mesosphere**

30 miles above the Earth

**Stratosphere**

**Ozone layer**

6 to 10 miles above the Earth

**Troposphere**

**Earth**

fires. Cleaning solutions, hair spray, and other common household products can also pollute the air with gas and tiny liquid droplets.

Air pollution is usually the worst in big cities with lots of cars and factories. But pollution doesn't stay in just the city or town where it originates. Air is always moving, and moving air (wind) carries pollution with it. Pollution does not stop at state or international borders. The wind needs no passport, and air pollution gets a free ride to the wind's destination. As a result, pollution has traveled all around the Earth. Places without cars, factories, or people have become polluted—even the North and South Poles.

This book will examine the connection between air pollution and the weather—factors such as sunshine, wind, clouds, rain, fog, and thunderstorms. We'll see what happens when pollution enters our skies, how pollution affects our health and the environment, how weather moves pollution from place to place, and, perhaps most importantly, what we can do to fight air pollution.

By-products from heavy industry account for much of our air pollution.

# 1.

# NOT A NEW PROBLEM

**A**ir pollution did not begin with the invention of cars or the building of factories in big cities. Air pollution has been around for millions of years.

In fact, pollutants often enter the air naturally. For example, when volcanoes erupt, they spew a gas called sulfur dioxide into the air. Ocean waves contain microscopic salt particles, which enter the air as wind blows across the water. Lightning often causes pollution by starting forest fires, which can darken the sky with thousands of tons of smoke.

Lightning creates pollution even when it doesn't cause fire. The great heat of a lightning strike (over 10,000° Fahrenheit) can split apart molecules (tiny particles) of nitrogen and oxygen gas in the air. The particles re-form as different, polluting gases—nitric oxide and nitrogen oxide. About 100 lightning flashes occur on Earth every second, and each year lightning produces more than 30 million tons of pollution.

Another natural form of pollution is dust—tiny particles of

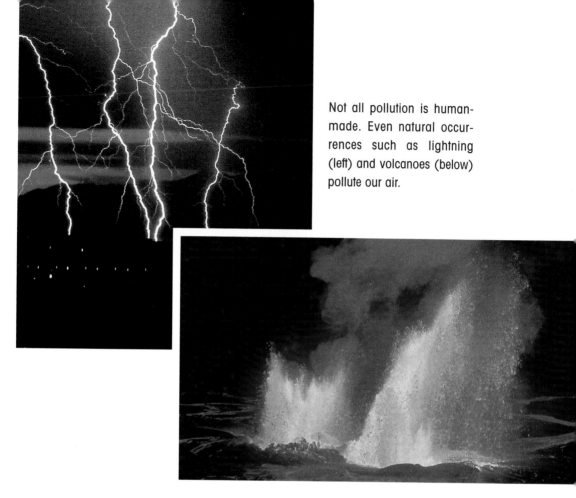

Not all pollution is human-made. Even natural occurrences such as lightning (left) and volcanoes (below) pollute our air.

soil. Dust enters the air when wind blows over deserts or other places that have few plants and roots to hold the soil in place. During droughts, periods of little or no rainfall, dry soil is easily picked up by strong winds.

## Nature's "Self-Cleaning Oven"

Once pollution has entered the air, it doesn't stay in the sky forever. Just as pollution often happens naturally, the atmosphere cleans itself naturally—sort of like a self-cleaning oven.

One result of wet deposition is the pollution of rivers, lakes, and oceans. This lake is no longer safe for human contact.

The main way in which the air cleans itself is by **deposition,** or dropping pollution to Earth. There are two kinds of deposition. *Wet deposition* occurs when rain or snow "washes" pollution from the sky to the Earth. The pollution might end up in a river, lake, or ocean, or it might seep into the ground with the rain.

*Dry deposition* occurs when polluted air strikes the Earth's surface. Air strikes the Earth all the time. Look at a tree swaying in the wind. Air is constantly bumping into the tree's leaves and branches. If the air hitting the tree is polluted, some of the pollution will leave the air and stick to the tree. This type of dry deposition is called *impaction.* Another type of dry deposition, called *settling,* occurs when pollution particles simply fall to Earth.

Even if there were no people on Earth, there would still be natural air pollution, and the atmosphere would clean itself naturally. But people add almost as much pollution to the air as natural sources do—sometimes more. The extra pollution from human sources is often too great for nature's "self-cleaning oven." And as the human population has increased, the problem has gotten worse.

## Fire: A Revolutionary Discovery

When humans first discovered how to create and control fire, life changed forever for the human race. Many prehistoric people lived in caves, which were dark and often cold. No one knows where or when people first learned to use fire. The first torch might have been a tree branch that had been set on fire by lightning.

Fire gave people light, warmth, and heat for cooking. But along with the benefits of fire came the unpleasant effects of air pollution. Fire brought thick billows of smelly black smoke, which could choke people in caves. When people began to build houses, they also built chimneys that carried some of the smoke out of their houses into the atmosphere.

People discovered many uses for fire. The great heat of a fire could harden clay pots and melt metal for toolmaking. To contain fires, people built ovens, fireplaces, and furnaces. These were stoked with fuels such as wood and coal.

When early peoples began to plant crops, they needed open fields. To clear the land, people often cut down trees and set them on fire. This "slash-and-burn" system of farming added a lot of smoke to the air. Even the cleared fields contributed to pollution. Without tree roots to hold the soil together, fields dried out and became dusty. Wind picked up the dust and lofted it into the atmosphere.

Over the centuries, as towns grew and became more crowded, air pollution became more irritating. In A.D. 61, the philosopher Seneca protested the "pestilential vapors and soot," the "stink of the smoky chimneys," and the "heavy air" of ancient Rome. In 1157, Eleanor of Aquitaine, the wife of King Henry II of England, called the smoky air of Nottingham Castle "unendurable" and packed her bags and moved out.

Burning coal fueled much of the Industrial Revolution. As a result, cities with heavy industry experienced severe air pollution.

Burning fuel became even more important during the Industrial Revolution, which began nearly 200 years ago. In Europe and the United States, the farming life gave way to a new world of manufacturing. People began to buy goods made in factories instead of making their own clothes and tools. Cities grew. Giant furnaces were stoked with coal. Great amounts of smoke belched out of factory chimneys.

## Sounding the Alarm

By 1900 urban pollution had become severe. Pittsburgh, Pennsylvania, an industrial city that produced steel, became known as "the Smoky City." Pollution was also severe in London, England, where smoky air from industry mixed with the heavy fog that often shrouds the London area. Harold Des Voiux, an English physician, combined the words smoke and fog and called this mixture "smog."

Doctors warned of the harmful effects of smoke on human lungs. But despite the health risks and the unpleasantness, people did little to combat increasing levels of smoke in the air. Business owners made a lot of money by running factories. They didn't want to scale back operations and burn less fuel.

More pollution came from car exhaust. The first cars, invented around 1900, were too expensive for most people. But, by the 1920s, cars were being mass-produced on assembly lines. Prices fell, and soon millions of people were driving their own cars. While cars made travel more convenient, they also released harmful pollutants into the air. One pollutant was lead, which came from gasoline, the liquid mixture that fueled the cars. By the end of World War II (1945), car exhaust had begun to cause pollution problems in Los Angeles.

Disaster struck in 1948. During a five-day period in October, a huge cloud of smoke lingered over the Monongahela River Valley in an industrial area of western Pennsylvania. Nearly half of the 14,000 residents of Donora, Pennsylvania, fell sick from the smoke. Twenty people died.

An even worse episode occurred in London in December 1952. A combination of thick fog, heavy smoke, and little wind to carry the pollution away claimed the lives of nearly 4,000 residents during a five-day period.

These disasters prompted the American and British governments to create laws controlling the amount of pollution that factories and cars could release into the atmosphere. In the United States, this legislation is called the Clean Air Act.

The Clean Air Act, created in 1970, requires each state to control and reduce air pollution. States set regulations that business and industry must follow. To comply with the Clean Air Act, manufacturers have installed **scrubbers,** devices that remove many harmful pollutants from smoke before it leaves factory smokestacks. Auto manufacturers have installed pollution-control devices called **catalytic converters** on cars. Catalytic converters change some of the harmful gases in car exhaust into harmless gases. Automakers have also switched to making cars that run on lead-free gasoline.

Individuals have tried to cut down on pollution too. When people carpool or ride buses and subways instead of driving alone, they burn less gasoline. Riding a bike or walking to

## SHRINKING FUEL SUPPLIES

A lot of air pollution comes from combustion, the burning of fossil fuels such as coal, oil, and natural gas. But our supply of fossil fuels is rapidly decreasing. At current rates of consumption, the Earth's oil reserves will be gone by the year 2040, and coal and natural gas reserves will last for only about 200 years.

Both air pollution and decreasing fossil fuel supplies have prompted people to look for alternative, cleaner forms of energy, such as solar and wind power. Unlike fossil fuels, sunshine and wind are plentiful on Earth.

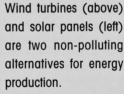

Wind turbines (above) and solar panels (left) are two non-polluting alternatives for energy production.

school doesn't add any pollution to the air. In polluted cities such as Los Angeles and Denver, city officials ask residents to avoid unnecessary driving on days when pollution levels are high.

Despite pollution-control efforts, billions of tons of pollutants are added to the atmosphere each year. Nearly a half billion tons of just one pollutant—sulfur—enter the atmosphere from both natural and human sources. Although this amount

Biking is a popular and healthful form of transportation that does not pollute the air.

Factories install scrubbers and other pollution-control devices (right) to remove harmful industrial pollutants before they enter the atmosphere. If not removed, these pollutants (above) become part of the air we breathe and return to our environment through wet and dry deposition.

sounds large, it is small when compared to the six quadrillion (6,000,000 billion) tons of air in the Earth's atmosphere. But that doesn't mean that air pollution isn't harmful. The more pollution we add to the air, the more we damage our environment and even our own health.

# 2

# POLLUTED SKIES

To operate machinery, industries burn fuel—usually coal, natural gas, or oil. Cars, trucks, boats, and buses run on gasoline. The furnaces that heat our homes, schools, and businesses operate by burning oil, coal, natural gas, or wood. The process of burning fuel is called **combustion.**

Combustion creates many harmful by-products, or pollutants. Some common pollutants are soot, ash, carbon monoxide, sulfur and nitrogen oxides, and poisonous metals such as lead and arsenic. The solid and liquid pollutants in the air are visible, taking the form of smoke. Gas pollution is invisible.

Air pollution is found in nearly all major cities on Earth. Los Angeles, Salt Lake City, Milwaukee, and Denver have the most serious air pollution problems in the United States. Pollution is so bad in Denver that residents often cannot see through the "brown cloud" in the sky to the spectacular Rocky Mountains west of the city. In Los Angeles, nearby mountain ranges can rarely be seen through the smog.

Small cities usually have fewer pollution problems than big ones. Cities that receive a lot of rain or snowfall sometimes have

Air pollution levels in cities such as New York are closely monitored.

### MEASURING AIR POLLUTION

Government agencies monitor air pollution levels in all major American cities. Monitoring takes place at selected buildings. Air from outside is pumped into the building through a tube called an inlet manifold. Inlet manifolds are made of glass, stainless steel, or other materials that won't participate in chemical reactions.

Once inside the building, the air is pumped into special instruments that measure ozone, nitrogen oxides, sulfur dioxide, and other pollutants. Pollution levels are recorded and relayed to the local air quality control office for analysis.

If pollution levels are high, public officials will notify the public of any danger. People may be advised to limit exercise, outdoor activities, or driving.

low pollution levels, since rain and snow wash pollution from the sky. Strong winds also help keep cities clean by blowing pollution away (but it may then bother people in another area).

## Pollution Far and Wide

It would be nice if we could say that the farther you go from a large city, the cleaner the air gets. While this statement is sometimes true, it isn't always so. Pollution travels with the wind. People living downwind of smelly businesses such as slaughterhouses and paper mills are well aware of this connection. In fact, rural areas directly downwind of industrial cities are often just as polluted as the cities themselves. The air over the Arctic Ocean is often very polluted, even though the closest big cities are thousands of miles away!

In poor countries such as China and Brazil, small villages are often more polluted than large cities. Pollution from nearby big cities isn't always at fault, however. In remote villages in poor nations, most power plants and factories do not have modern pollution-control devices. These plants and factories often create more harmful pollutants than urban industries. To make matters worse, many poor countries do not have effective pollution-control laws.

Some pollution problems are unique to rural areas. One common rural pollutant is dust. Cars and trucks driving on dirt roads raise dust. So does wind passing over tilled fields. During severe droughts, winds may loft huge amounts of dust into the air. Dust storms may blacken the sky and coat roads, fields, and houses with a layer of fine sand. When drought plagued the

Great Plains in the 1930s, strong winds whipped up tons of dust. Millions of acres of farmland were destroyed. The region became known as the "Dust Bowl."

## A Laboratory in the Sky

The atmosphere is made of many gases—about 78 percent is nitrogen, about 21 percent is oxygen, and between 1 and 4 percent is **water vapor** (water in gas form). Other gases are found in smaller amounts. The atmosphere also contains water droplets and ice crystals, which are found inside clouds.

All this gas and water, combined with heat and light from the Sun, make the atmosphere a natural chemical laboratory. Millions of **chemical reactions** occur in the atmosphere every second. A chemical reaction is a process in which one substance, such as a gas, is changed to another substance. For instance, nitrogen and oxygen may combine to form nitric oxide and nitrogen dioxide during a lightning strike. Pollutants in the atmosphere take part in chemical reactions too.

Pollutants that enter the atmosphere directly from cars, households, industry, and natural sources are called **primary pollutants.** Once in the atmosphere's "natural laboratory," primary pollutants often react with water, sunlight, or other gases to form new kinds of pollution. Pollutants that result from chemical reactions in the atmosphere are called **secondary pollutants.**

For example, when nitric oxide enters the air from cars and smokestacks, it may combine with oxygen in a series of chemical reactions. The result is a secondary pollutant called **ozone.**

Ozone is desirable high in the atmosphere, in the ozone layer, where it protects us from the Sun's harmful rays. But at ground level, ozone is harmful, causing both breathing and heart problems.

Many chemical reactions, such as the ones that create ozone, require sunlight and warm temperatures. This fact explains why the worst ozone pollution occurs in sunny areas with lots of primary pollution. Los Angeles and Mexico City are good examples. Cold weather cities such as Chicago and Milwaukee have ozone pollution only in summertime.

Sulfuric acid is another secondary pollutant. It is created when sulfur in the air (from the burning of coal, oil, or natural gas) combines with oxygen and water vapor. Sulfuric acid creates a milky white haze in the sky. This haze reduces visibility (the distance people can see). Haze is a problem for airplane pilots and sometimes for visitors at scenic areas, such as the Grand Canyon.

When nitrogen dioxide, nitric oxide, or sulfur dioxide combines with water inside a cloud, the result is nitric acid or sulfuric acid. If rain or snow falls from the cloud, these acids travel to the ground. This type of secondary pollution is called **acid rain.** It can harm plants and animals, especially those that live in water.

Just as chemical reactions can change primary pollutants into secondary pollutants, chemical reactions can also change primary and secondary pollutants into harmless gases. Ozone, for example, reacts easily to produce many other gases—some of them harmful and others harmless.

Chemical reactions, along with wet and dry deposition, are part of the atmosphere's natural cleaning process. Unfortunately, this process is neither thorough nor fast enough to protect us from air pollution. People constantly breathe polluted air, even while it is being cleaned.

These leaves show severe damage caused by acid rain.

3

# NEGATIVE
# EFFECTS

People burn fuel to provide themselves with heat, transportation, and manufactured goods. These things make our lives more comfortable. But the same processes that make human life easier can also hurt people and the environment. The air pollution that results from heating, automobile travel, and manufacturing can cause illness—even death. Animals, plants, and even buildings can be hurt by air pollution as well.

## Hazardous to Your Health

The hairs that line our nose and the sticky mucus that lines our upper respiratory (breathing) system are designed to filter out foreign particles when we breathe. When the respiratory system is irritated, we usually cough or sneeze to expel the contaminating material.

Years of exposure to pollution can break down the body's natural protection, however. Respiratory diseases can result.

## SMOG CITY

Southern California has the worst smog problem in the United States. More than 9,000,000 motor vehicles, as well as thousands of industries, pollute the skies of Los Angeles and nearby communities. Steady sea breezes carry the pollution inland, where it is trapped by surrounding mountain ranges. Sunshine, warm temperatures, and temperature inversions create a "smog factory" in which primary pollution reacts chemically to produce secondary pollution.

Daily weather reports on TV and in the newspaper give residents of Los Angeles detailed information on air quality. The reports include predicted levels of ozone, nitrogen dioxide, and carbon monoxide. If pollution levels are high, city officials will issue a Stage I smog alert. People are told to avoid vigorous exercise. A Stage II alert means that air quality is extremely poor and people should avoid all physical exercise. A Stage III alert signals hazardous conditions during which everyone should remain indoors.

People in Los Angeles are working together to clean up their air. Nearly 2,000,000 residents ride in carpools, use public transportation, or bicycle to work each day. Businesses can be fined up to $50,000 per day for breaking pollution-control laws. These efforts have cut the number of Stage I alerts in half since the mid-1980s. Stage II alerts, which used to occur 15 times a year, have become rare. Despite these improvements, the air in Los Angeles is still rated at Stage I about 120 days of the year.

Some common respiratory diseases are asthma, bronchitis, emphysema, and lung cancer.

Certain pollutants are particularly dangerous. Carbon monoxide, a major part of car exhaust, prevents the delivery of oxygen to the body's cells. If a person breathes high levels of carbon monoxide, the first symptoms are headache, fatigue, and drowsiness. Long exposure can lead to death.

Benzene, a common industrial cleaning solution, is thought to cause cancer. Nitrogen dioxide and nitric oxide can create or aggravate heart problems. Ozone can damage the heart and lungs. In Los Angeles, many people avoid outdoor exercise during times of high ozone pollution because increased breathing rates will bring more of the harmful chemical into their body.

## Wildlife in Danger

Some pollutants, especially ozone, nitrogen dioxide, and sulfur dioxide, damage plants when they enter the pores (tiny holes) in leaves. Air pollution can damage and kill crops. Wheat, corn, soybeans, and peanuts are especially vulnerable. In the United States, pollution destroys $2 billion to $5 billion in crops each year and reduces food production by 5 to 10 percent.

Many tree leaves and needles have a waxy coating that prevents water loss during droughts and offers protection from frost and insects. Pollution breaks down this coating and makes trees vulnerable to damage and disease. Pollution frequently kills trees and plants around factories and power plants, creating a desolate, lifeless landscape nearby.

Acid pollution is particularly damaging to forests and animal

Destruction caused by acid rain is evident in this New England forest.

life. In addition to damaging leaves, acid from both wet deposition (acid rain) and dry deposition draws poisonous minerals such as aluminum and magnesium out of the forest soil. These minerals can cause disease in both plants and animals.

When acid rain or acid snow falls or rolls into a lake or stream, aluminum and other minerals are drawn out of rocks and sediment at the bottom of the water. These minerals are toxic to the plants that live in water. The minerals also kill fish by causing their gills to clog with mucus. During the first warm days of spring, as winter snow melts, a lot of acidic water may rush into a lake or stream. This process is called **acidification** or "acid shock."

These historic structures show the damaging effects of air pollution and acid rain—pitting, discoloration, and deterioration.

More than 20,000 lakes in the United States and Canada have been harmed by acid rain. Surprisingly, acidified lakes often look strangely beautiful, with water so crystal clear that you can see through it to the bottom. But don't be fooled by this false beauty—the water is clear because nothing is alive in it, not even the tiny plants called algae that darken the color of healthy lakes.

## Urban Destruction

Air pollution can cause serious damage when it comes in contact with human-made structures. Both wet deposition (acid rain and snow) and dry deposition carry destructive chemicals to Earth. Damage typically occurs over many years of exposure. Sulfur dioxide can be particularly harmful. It can pit and discolor stone, corrode metal, eat away paint on cars and houses, and soil flags and clothing. In the United States, damage to buildings from air pollution is estimated at $5 billion a year.

In the old cities of Europe, pollution over many centuries has damaged marble statues, stained-glass windows, castles, and other historic buildings. In many polluted cities, people periodically clean the outsides of buildings to remove the soot.

Because air from outside sometimes comes inside, air pollution can also damage indoor materials. Books, in particular, are vulnerable. Certain kinds of pollutants, especially sulfur dioxide, erode leather bindings and harden and crack paper. Some libraries store old and rare books in special sulfur dioxide–free containers to prevent such damage.

# 4

# THE ROLE OF WEATHER

If you've ever ridden on a school or city bus, you know that you can only go where the bus takes you. Wind is like a bus system for air pollution: the pollution goes where the wind carries it.

The prevailing winds, great wind belts that circle the Earth, carry pollution long distances. Summertime travelers to the Grand Canyon National Park in Arizona are sometimes disappointed to find that haze in the sky prevents them from seeing the park's gorgeous vistas. Why? A wind belt called the prevailing westerlies often carries hazy air from the Los Angeles area into the Grand Canyon region hundreds of miles to the east. (People living in Hawaii are grateful for the westerlies. Since the westerlies circle the Earth from west to east, dirty air from Los Angeles never travels westward to Hawaii.)

Local winds also carry pollution, but not as far. Local winds are controlled by a simple principle: warm air rises and cold air sinks. Think of a mountain valley. During the day, sunshine

Air pollution causes a haze that often obscures scenic views of the Grand Canyon.

warms the valley. The air in the valley heats up and begins to flow up the mountain, creating a "valley breeze." (Winds are named for the direction or place from which they blow.) At night, the situation reverses. The land cools, and cool air sinks into the valley, creating a "mountain breeze."

In mountainous or hilly areas, cities and towns are usually located in valleys. During the day, the valley breeze can carry air pollution from a city's factories and automobiles up the

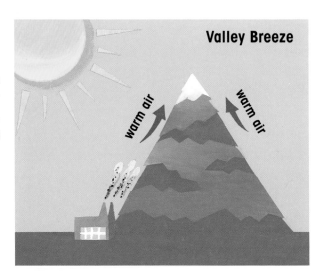

**Valley Breeze**

warm air

warm air

A *valley breeze* occurs when sunshine heats air at lower elevations during the day. The hot air rises and carries pollutants upward.

**Mountain Breeze**

cool air

cool air

At night, the air cools and settles into the valleys. Polluted air is trapped in the valley by this *mountain breeze.*

mountain, away from people. But at night, a mountain breeze can trap polluted air inside the valley. If you were in charge of controlling pollution in a valley town with several factories, when would you allow the factories to burn fuel—during the day or at night?

## Sea Breeze / Land Breeze

Land heats up (and cools down) faster than water does. This fact won't come as a surprise to you if you ever go swimming in a lake or ocean. The water can sometimes be quite cold, even when the beach is hot.

During the day, sunshine warms the land, and hot air above the land rises. The water stays cool, however, and cool air over the water begins to sink. Sinking air is under high **pressure.** To understand high pressure, imagine that a giant hand above the water is pushing the cool air downward. When the sinking air hits the water, the air can't go any farther down, so it turns and moves sideways. It rushes toward the land to replace the warm air that is rising. This rushing air is called the "sea breeze" (or "lake breeze" along the shores of large lakes).

Again, the situation reverses at night. Land cools more quickly than water does. This time, the cool air above the land is under high pressure. It sinks toward the ground and then rushes toward the water, creating a "land breeze."

Many factories and electric power plants are built along shorelines. The sea and land breezes have a big effect on air pollution levels near these facilities. Air pollution from coastal factories may travel over the water at night (following the land breeze) only to be brought back to land by the sea breeze during the day.

Northeastern Wisconsin, along the western shore of Lake

Michigan, is a mostly rural area that doesn't generate much pollution itself. Yet, in summertime, ozone pollution there is quite high. The cause is a southerly wind that carries primary pollutants northward from the industrial cities of Milwaukee, Chicago, and Gary. Most of the polluted air ends up over

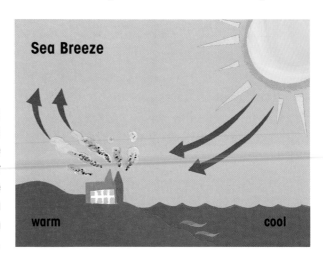

A *sea breeze* occurs during the day as cool air sitting over water sinks. When the air hits the water, the air moves sideways toward the shore. The resulting sea breeze carries air pollution from coastal factories inland.

At night, cool air above the land sinks and moves sideways toward the water. This *land breeze* carries pollution out over the sea.

Lake Michigan, where it undergoes chemical reactions that produce ozone. The daytime sea breeze carries the ozone over land, where it may harm Wisconsin residents.

## Vertical Motions

The term *wind* usually refers to the horizontal, or sideways, movement of air. But air can also move vertically—up and down. The atmosphere's up-and-down movements are very important in determining air pollution levels.

**Stability** refers to the amount of up-and-down motion in the air. During *unstable* conditions, a lot of air is rising and sinking. Bright sunshine can make air unstable. Here's why: As

Thunderstorms can form during unstable conditions.

sunlight heats the ground, the ground warms the air above it. Warm air rises. This rising motion creates a sort of "hole" in the atmosphere, and colder air from above sinks down to fill it.

When we're talking about air pollution, unstable conditions are good news. Vertical motions "mix" the air, spreading pollution (diluting it) over a large vertical area. As more pollution travels upward, less pollution remains to bother people on the ground.

Thunderstorms often form when the atmosphere is very unstable. Powerful storm clouds measure up to 10 miles from top to bottom. The clouds are tall because the air's vertical motions are extreme. Inside thunderstorms, air from ground level rises miles above the Earth. The rising air can carry pollution high into the atmosphere.

Friction—the rubbing of air against hills, trees, ocean waves, and buildings—slows the wind at ground level. But miles above the ground, where there are no objects to create friction, the wind is usually much stronger. During unstable conditions such as thunderstorms, when pollution reaches high altitudes, it may be carried away by these strong winds. In addition, the heavy rains of a thunderstorm wash a lot of pollution out of the sky.

## Stability and Stagnation

*Stable* conditions are bad news when it comes to air pollution. Stable conditions mean there is little vertical movement in the air. The lack of mixing can cause pollution levels to become more concentrated at ground level.

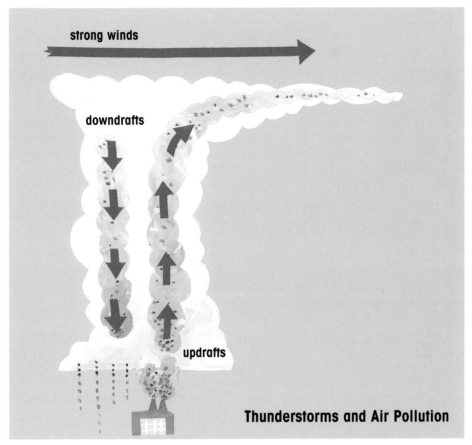

**strong winds**

**downdrafts**

**updrafts**

**Thunderstorms and Air Pollution**

The rising motion of air during thunderstorms pulls polluted air from factories up and away from land and people. It is then carried away by strong winds at higher elevations. Some pollution is washed from the sky by heavy rains.

Stable conditions occur when ground-level temperatures are not much greater than temperatures at high altitudes. Normally, because the Earth holds a lot of heat from the Sun, air at ground level is warmer than air high in the atmosphere.

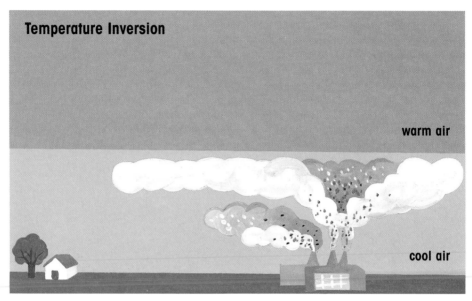

**Temperature Inversion**

warm air

cool air

A temperature inversion may occur during stable conditions on cold, clear nights. When air at ground level becomes cooler than air at higher elevations, it does not rise. Pollution spreads out horizontally. It is not carried to higher elevations by rising air.

At night, though, as the Earth cools off, temperatures at different levels of the atmosphere may even out. On very cold, clear nights, ground-level temperatures might become even lower than temperatures at high altitudes. This condition is called a **temperature inversion.**

Temperature inversions cause extreme stability. If the air near the ground is cold, it does not rise. If the air is polluted, the pollution spreads out horizontally and can build in intensity.

Another kind of temperature inversion occurs in **high pressure systems,** large areas of sinking air. Again, since the air is sinking, not rising, pollution stays near the ground. High pressure systems are often found in Southern California in summer. The high pressure creates temperature inversions that contribute to Los Angeles's serious pollution problem.

If stable conditions (little or no vertical air movement) combine with **stagnation** (little or no wind), one of the worst combinations for air pollution can result. When the air is stagnant, pollutants will not be carried away by the wind. If stable conditions and stagnation combine in an area with lots of pollution, the results can be tragic. The 1948 Donora disaster in

Weather balloons allow scientists to obtain information from high in the atmosphere.

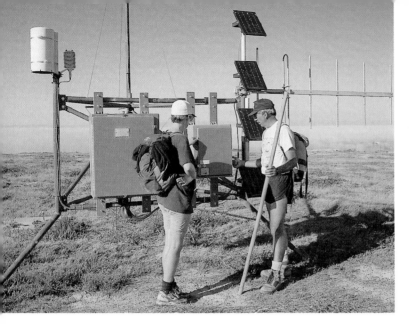

Land-based equipment also supplies crucial information about weather conditions.

Pennsylvania resulted from stable conditions, stagnation, and heavy pollution.

**Meteorologists** (scientists who study and predict the weather) determine stability by comparing temperatures at different altitudes. They use special instruments, such as weather balloons, to make their measurements. The rest of us can determine stability by using a simple technique: watching smoke from smokestacks. When smoke plumes are flat, we know there is little rising or sinking movement in the air—conditions are stable. When smoke plumes loop up and down, however, we know there is considerable up-and-down air movement, an indication of unstable conditions.

Though unstable conditions often carry pollution high into the atmosphere, away from people on the ground, the pollution hasn't completely gone away. From high in the atmosphere, the pollution may travel with the wind—sometimes far from the source of pollution.

## CHANGING THE WEATHER

We know how the weather can affect pollution. But did you know that pollution can even affect the weather?

Take a look at fog. Fog is a cloud that forms at ground level. Clouds form when water vapor in the air turns into liquid water. This process is called condensation.

When water vapor condenses, it collects around tiny particles called condensation nuclei. Normally, condensation nuclei are natural particles such as soil, dust, and salt from ocean spray.

In polluted cities, though, there are often more pollution particles than natural particles in the air. Some of these particles—sulfuric and nitric acid droplets, for instance—make good condensation nuclei. The abundance of pollution particles sometimes causes fog to form on days when the sky would be clear if the air were clean.

Fog forms at ground level when water vapor in the air turns to liquid.

# 5.

# OZONE DESTRUCTION

A pollutant's lifetime is the amount of time the pollutant stays in the air before it is removed. Removal can take place through a chemical reaction (in which the pollutant is changed into something else, perhaps a harmless gas) or by wet or dry deposition. Most pollutants, including ozone and airborne acids, have lifetimes of two weeks or less. But some pollutants have longer lifetimes—months or even years.

One group of pollutants, **chlorofluorocarbons (CFCs)**, have very long lifetimes. CFCs do not dissolve in water, so they aren't washed to the ground with rain. They don't usually participate in chemical reactions that would change them into different types of gases, either. As a result, CFCs can stay in the sky for a long time—up to 60 years.

CFCs were first developed in the 1930s as cleaning fluids for electronic equipment. Over the years, CFCs have been used in refrigerators, air conditioners, and foam packaging materials,

Liquid CFCs used as propellants in spray cans change to a gas and end up in the atmosphere. There they contribute to destruction of the ozone layer. When used in foam packaging materials, such as those shown here, CFCs help make the package stable and unlikely to decompose. Because of their negative effects on our environment, CFC production has been banned in the U.S. and many other nations.

and as propellants in spray cans. When CFCs are under pressure (such as inside a spray can), they take the form of a liquid. When CFCs are released into the atmosphere (during spraying, for instance), they take the form of a gas.

CFCs were designed to be noncorrosive—meaning they wouldn't dissolve or damage the material being cleaned—and nontoxic—not harmful to people who used them. They were also supposed to be nonreactive, meaning they wouldn't participate in chemical reactions.

The inventors of CFCs succeeded in developing a noncorrosive, nontoxic material. Unfortunately, the third condition, that the chemicals be nonreactive, didn't work out as well. We now know that CFCs *can* participate in chemical reactions if certain conditions are met: The temperature must be below –108°F, the Sun must be shining, and ice must be present. Under these conditions, CFCs take part in chemical reactions that lead to the destruction of large amounts of ozone.

No problem, right? No place on Earth has such low temperatures, ice, and sunshine all at the same time, right? Wrong. In the atmosphere over Antarctica, 15 miles above the Earth, this strange combination of extreme cold, sunlight, and ice can be found. And in a section of the atmosphere called the stratosphere—also 15 miles above the Earth—is where we find the ozone layer.

## Chemical Reactions

Antarctica is in the Southern Hemisphere. During its winter (which takes place during the Northern Hemisphere's summer),

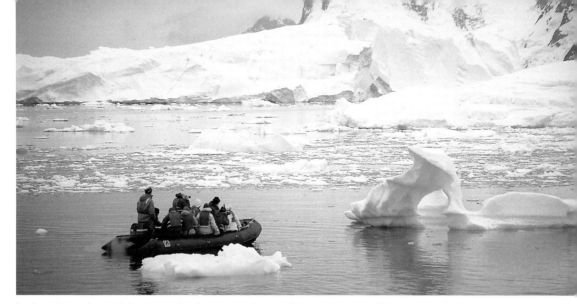

In the atmosphere high above the frozen continent of Antarctica, conditions are right for destruction of the ozone layer.

the Southern Hemisphere tilts away from the Sun, and the South Pole receives very little sunlight. As a result, the already-cold continent gets colder and colder. Temperatures in the stratosphere drop below –112°F. At this temperature, polar stratospheric clouds form miles above the Earth's surface. These clouds are made of microscopic ice crystals.

When sunlight returns to Antarctica in mid-September, the conditions for large-scale ozone destruction are suddenly met. In the intense cold of the Antarctic stratosphere, on the surface of millions of microscopic ice crystals bathed in sunlight, chemical reactions involving CFCs begin. The ozone begins to break down, leaving a "hole" in the ozone layer.

This hole doesn't stay open all year long. As sunlight continues to warm the Antarctic stratosphere in spring, temperatures slowly rise. By November, temperatures generally reach above –108°F. This temperature is too high for the polar

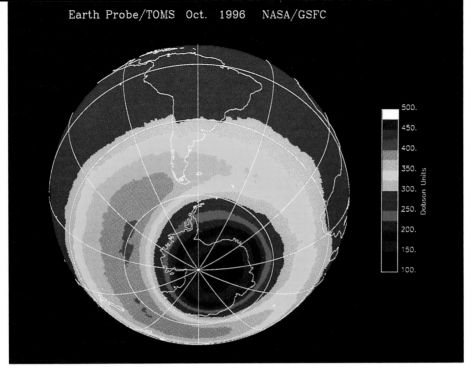

The Total Ozone Mapping Spectrometer (TOMS) measures ozone levels in our atmosphere. The ozone hole over Antarctica, shown here in black, forms in September and remains until the end of November.

stratospheric clouds. The ice crystals inside the clouds turn into water vapor, and ozone destruction stops—only to begin again the next year.

The scientists who invented CFCs probably didn't think that CFCs would end up 15 miles above the South Pole. After all, there are no cities or factories in Antarctica. Very few people live there—only small groups of scientists. How did CFCs get to Antarctica? They were carried by the wind.

It takes weeks or even months for CFCs from the United States and other industrialized nations to reach the South Pole. But CFCs have lifetimes of many years. They have plenty of time to make the journey.

Global wind patterns also carry CFCs to the other end of the Earth—to the North Pole. But because temperatures at the North Pole aren't as low as those at the South Pole, ozone destruction there is not as severe.

## Why Worry?

While ozone near the ground can damage our health, ozone high in the atmosphere, in the ozone layer, protects us. The ozone layer filters out **ultraviolet (UV) radiation** from the Sun. UV radiation can cause skin cancer and eye disease.

People are already feeling the negative effects of ozone destruction. In recent years, skin cancer rates have increased in countries close to Antarctica. In Australia, children are required to wear sunscreen when they go to school.

Ozone destruction threatens plants and animals too. UV radiation can damage and even kill microscopic sea creatures called plankton. Since larger sea animals feed on plankton, UV radiation ultimately threatens the food supply of all living things in Antarctica.

Scientists first measured dropping ozone levels above the South Pole in the 1970s. Since then, the United States and many other countries have banned the production of CFCs. Ozone levels in the stratosphere continue to drop, however, because CFCs have such long lifetimes. Despite new laws, CFCs continue to leak out of old air conditioners, refrigerators, and other products. In addition, some countries have not banned CFCs. If all countries were to eliminate CFCs, ozone would begin to build up naturally in the ozone layer sometime during the 21st century.

6

# A WARMING TREND

**A**t thousands of weather stations around the world, meteorologists measure and record wind speed, temperature, rainfall, snowfall, and other weather features. By comparing measurements over many years, meteorologists have noticed a trend—over the past 100 years, average worldwide temperatures have increased by 1° Fahrenheit.

One degree may not sound like a big increase. But some scientists think that a continued warming trend could cause droughts, heat waves, and other weather extremes. Even a small increase in average temperatures might melt ice in polar regions, scientists believe. The melting would increase the water level in oceans and possibly lead to widespread flooding of coastal cities.

Why have temperatures increased? No one knows for sure, but some scientists think air pollution has played a role in the increase. Their theory also involves a natural process known as the **greenhouse effect.**

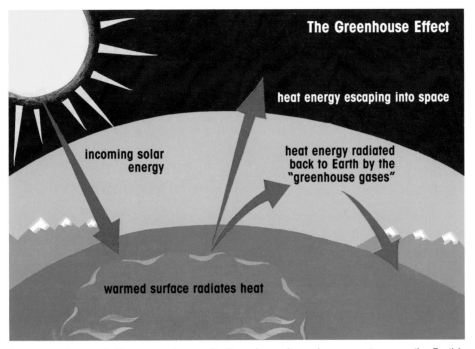

The Greenhouse Effect

incoming solar energy

heat energy escaping into space

heat energy radiated back to Earth by the "greenhouse gases"

warmed surface radiates heat

Our atmosphere acts like a greenhouse. It allows incoming solar energy to warm the Earth's surface. Heat energy from the Earth is then radiated back toward space. Some of this heat energy escapes directly into space. However, some heat energy is absorbed by the "greenhouse gases" in the atmosphere and is radiated toward the Earth, keeping the surface comfortably warm.

Certain gases in the atmosphere help warm the Earth in much the same way as a greenhouse warms the plants inside. These gases allow sunlight to pass through to the Earth. But, like glass in a greenhouse, the gases don't allow much heat to pass back out of the atmosphere. The gases act like a blanket, holding heat near the Earth. One gas that plays an important role in the greenhouse effect is carbon dioxide.

This forest is being cleared using the slash-and-burn method.

## More Carbon Dioxide

Carbon dioxide makes up less than 1 percent of the Earth's atmosphere. Yet it is important to life on Earth. Plants can't live without carbon dioxide. Plants convert carbon dioxide (along with water and sunlight) into glucose, a kind of sugar that helps them grow.

Since the early 1800s, carbon dioxide levels on Earth have increased by 25 percent. Levels continue to increase each year. The cause is people. We have added carbon dioxide to the atmosphere in several ways. First of all, combustion (the burning of fuels) creates carbon dioxide. Secondly, since pre-agricultural times, people have cleared away much of the Earth's forested area. Trees have been cut to make room for houses, farms, and cities. The clearing of the Earth's forested regions is called **deforestation.**

What happens after people cut down forests? For one thing,

the trees (since they're dead) no longer take carbon dioxide from the air. In addition, the cut trees are often burned (by the slash-and-burn method of clearing a field). Deforestation thus doubly adds to carbon dioxide pollution: The chopped-down trees no longer take carbon dioxide from the air, and the burning process adds more carbon dioxide to the air. Carbon dioxide has a lifetime of about five years. So the effects of slashing and burning last long after the fires die down.

Deforestation continues. One-half of the remaining forests on Earth are in tropical regions. Human populations in these regions are growing quickly, and about 70 billion acres of tropical rain forests are cleared each year to make room for increasing numbers of people. As more rain forests come down, carbon dioxide levels continue to rise.

## Cause and Effect

Let's think about the greenhouse effect again and consider a simple cause-and-effect theory: (1) The greenhouse effect keeps the Earth warm. (2) Carbon dioxide makes the greenhouse effect stronger. (3) Carbon dioxide levels are increasing. (4) The Earth is growing warmer.

Using this theory, it's easy to conclude that increased carbon dioxide levels—from deforestation and combustion—cause global warming. To keep temperatures from rising further, some scientists say, we should stop rain forest destruction and burn less fuel.

Other scientists disagree. They point to several factors beyond the "cause-and-effect" theory. By studying ancient tree rings, ice from polar regions, and sediment beneath the oceans, scientists have determined that global temperatures have changed (both upward and downward) by much more than 1° Fahrenheit many times during the past 800,000 years. Combustion could not have caused ancient global warming and cooling because there were no industrial civilizations hundreds of thousands of years ago. Nor was there widespread deforestation.

So natural factors—possibly changes in the Earth's orbit around the Sun—must have caused the warming and cooling. If natural factors created global warming and cooling in the past, perhaps the most recent global warming has a natural cause unrelated to industrial activity.

The debate over global warming is further complicated by

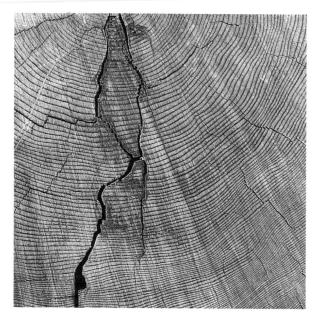

Scientists can determine past temperature changes by studying ancient tree rings.

weather factors. In a world with rising temperatures, more water will evaporate from the oceans (heat turns liquid water into water vapor). More water vapor leads to more clouds. Increased cloud cover blocks sunlight and shades the Earth, which leads to falling temperatures. We have global warming now. But could global cooling be just around the corner?

## Looking at the Data

The news that the Earth is warming comes from weather stations that have been taking temperature readings for the past 100 years or so, and most weather stations are located in cities. Cities have grown in the past 100 years. Because concrete and buildings heat up faster than grass, shrubs, and trees, cities are often warmer than the surrounding countryside. Is it possible that higher temperature readings are due to the growth of cities rather than to changes in the atmosphere? Some scientists think so.

Is global warming caused by a buildup of carbon dioxide in the atmosphere or is it a more complex phenomenon involving natural and human-made processes? We don't yet know. To find the answer, scientists perform experiments, measure pollution levels in the atmosphere with airplanes, ships, and satellites, and analyze a vast amount of information with powerful computers.

Some people think that since we don't know for sure if air pollution is causing global warming, we shouldn't bother trying to burn less fuel or save our forests. Other people believe that even if air pollution is not causing global warming, it's still a good idea to reduce pollution and make a healthier environment. What do you think?

# 7.

# THE NEXT STEP?

**C**an we preserve the quality of our atmosphere? Can we clean up polluted areas and prevent or reduce future pollution? The job will involve government, scientists, and ordinary people working together.

The Montreal Protocol is one example of governments working to fight air pollution. In 1987, representatives from 24 nations met in Montreal, Canada, and agreed to pass laws that would gradually reduce CFC levels. Two years later, representatives from nearly 90 countries met in Copenhagen, Denmark, to strengthen the agreement.

The Clean Air Act also shows us how government can fight pollution. Since the act went into effect in 1970, levels of sulfur dioxide, carbon monoxide, lead, and other pollutants have dropped significantly in the United States. Cars of the 1990s produce 20 times less pollution than cars of the 1970s. Ozone-pollution levels are still high, however.

In 1990 Congress revised the Clean Air Act, in an effort to reduce levels of sulfur dioxide, the major cause of acid rain and haze. Under the new law, electric power plants that reduce

## ACID FOG

Fog is a cloud that forms near the Earth's surface.

Fog that contains pollutants such as sulfuric acid and nitric acid is called acid fog. Acid fog is even more damaging to wildlife than acid rain, because the acid in cloud droplets is more concentrated than acid in rainwater. In other words, the ratio of acid to water is greater in acid fog.

When acid fog is present, acids from cloud droplets are deposited directly on trees. Acid fog poses a special threat to plant and animal life in many mountainous areas. For instance, forests in the Appalachian Mountains, a range downwind of many large industrial areas in the eastern United States, have been damaged by acid fog.

Acid fog is more destructive to plants and animals than acid rain.

emissions (discharges) of sulfur dioxide receive a tax break. Acid rain has decreased in parts of the United States since 1990. But it still threatens many lakes, streams, and forests.

## NUCLEAR ALTERNATIVE

Nuclear energy, which is created by splitting atoms of uranium and plutonium, can provide enormous amounts of electricity without polluting the air. About 7 percent of the world's electricity comes from nuclear energy.

At first glance, nuclear energy looks like a good alternative to combustion, but it has many drawbacks. Nuclear power plants are expensive to build and operate safely. Used nuclear fuel (nuclear waste) is radioactive and poses great dangers to human health and the environment. Nuclear waste is difficult to store or dispose of safely.

Although nuclear power doesn't create air pollution under normal conditions, accidents at nuclear power plants can create dangerous radioactive pollution. On April 25, 1986, explosions at the Chernobyl nuclear power plant in the Ukraine flung large amounts of radioactive chemicals into the air. Within weeks, the pollution had spread over the globe. It was even found at the South Pole. By 1994, more than 8,000 people had died from exposure to the Chernobyl pollution. After the disaster, scientists commented that "a major nuclear accident anywhere is a nuclear accident everywhere."

People are also trying to fight air pollution by finding new ways to produce energy. Much of our energy supply (electricity, heat, and light) is created by combustion. But since combustion creates a lot of air pollution, scientists have developed alternative, cleaner energy sources. One example is hydroelectric power—electricity generated by moving water (usually rivers). Wind turbines (giant windmills) are another alternative. They harness the power of the wind to create electricity. Solar energy systems capture the power of the Sun for both heat and electricity. Alternative technologies such as these provide less than 10 percent of the world's energy supply, though they may account for a bigger percentage in the future.

You can help control pollution by recycling and conserving fuel. When you recycle metal, paper, plastic, and glass, you reduce the amount of fuel required to make more of these materials. Driving in carpools, turning off lights when you leave a room, turning your furnace down a little in winter—these are just a few of the many steps you can take to use less fuel and fight pollution.

Cutting down on air pollution will not be easy, but preserving the quality of our atmosphere is worth the effort. People like you can play a vital part. By learning about the relationship between pollution, weather, and the environment, you've taken an important step. Now it's time to put your knowledge to work. What sources of pollution exist where you live? What can you do to protect the air we breathe? What is your community doing? Your actions can help lead the way to a brighter, healthier future for our environment.

# GLOSSARY

**acidification:** the sudden addition of large amounts of acid, from rain or snow, into a lake or stream

**acid rain:** rain containing acid such as nitric acid or sulfuric acid

**air pollution:** contamination of the air

**atmosphere:** the blanket of gas that surrounds the Earth

**catalytic converters:** pollution-control devices on cars that change harmful gases from car exhaust into harmless ones

**chemical reaction:** a process in which one substance, such as a gas, is changed to another substance

**chlorofluorocarbons (CFCs):** substances used in manufacturing that undergo chemical reactions in the atmosphere, resulting in the destruction of ozone

**combustion:** the process of burning fuel

**deforestation:** the clearing of large forested regions on Earth

**deposition:** the transfer of pollutants from the air to the Earth

**greenhouse effect:** a natural process that keeps the Earth warm. The process involves gases such as carbon dioxide that allow the Sun's heat to enter the atmosphere but do not allow much heat from the Earth to escape back into space.

**high pressure system:** a large area of sinking air

**meteorologists:** scientists who study and predict the weather

**ozone:** a secondary pollutant created when primary pollutants such as nitric oxide or nitrogen dioxide react with oxygen in the air. Ozone is also created naturally in the stratosphere.

**ozone layer:** a portion of the stratosphere, about 15 miles above the ground, containing high levels of ozone. The ozone layer absorbs harmful ultraviolet rays given off by the Sun.

**pressure:** the force of air pressing against the Earth's surface

**primary pollutant:** a pollutant that enters the air directly from cars, factories, households, or other sources

**scrubbers:** devices that remove harmful pollutants from factory smokestacks before they are released into the air

**secondary pollutant:** pollution created by a chemical reaction involving a primary pollutant

**stability:** the amount of vertical motion in the air

**stagnation:** little or no wind

**temperature inversion:** a condition in which air near the ground is cooler than air at higher altitudes

**ultraviolet radiation:** harmful energy from the Sun

**water vapor:** water in gas form

# INDEX

acid, 7, 28–29, 44, 57
acidification, 29, 31
acid rain, 24, 29, 31
air. *See* atmosphere
air pollution, defined, 7
aluminum, 29
animals and air pollution, 7, 24, 29, 49
Antarctica, 46–49
arsenic, 20
ash, 20
atmosphere, 6; layers of, 8; natural cleaning of, 11–13. *See also* stable air conditions; unstable air conditions
Australia, 49

benzene, 28
books and air pollution, 7, 31
buildings and air pollution, 7, 31

carbon dioxide, 52–53
carbon monoxide, 7, 20, 27, 28, 56
car exhaust, 7, 15–16, 28
catalytic converters, 16
cause and effect theory, 53–55
chemical reactions, 7, 23–25, 44, 46–49
chlorofluorocarbons (CFCs), 44–49
cigarette smoke, 7
Clean Air Act, 16, 56–57
combustion, 17, 20, 52, 54, 59

deforestation, 52–53, 54
Denver, Colorado, 18, 20
deposition, 12. *See also* dry deposition; wet deposition
droughts, 11, 22–23, 28
dry deposition, 12, 25, 29, 31, 44
dust, 6, 10–11, 14, 22

factories, 7, 15, 16, 22, 28, 35
farming, 13–14, 28, 53
fire, 13–15
fireplaces, 7
fog, 15, 16, 43, 57
forest fires, 7, 9, 10
fossil fuels, 17
friction, 38

global warming, 50–55
greenhouse effect, 50–53

health concerns, 15–19, 26, 27, 28
high pressure systems, 35, 40–41
household furnaces, 7
household products, 9
hydroelectric power, 59

impactation, 12
Industrial Revolution, 15
inlet manifold, 21

land breeze, 35–36
lead, 7, 15, 20, 56
lightning, 10, 11, 23
London, England, 15, 16
Los Angeles, California, 16, 18, 20, 24, 27, 28, 41

measuring air pollution, 21
mesosphere, 8
meteorologists, 41, 42, 50
meteors, 6
Milwaukee, Wisconsin, 20, 24
Montreal Protocol, 56
mountain breeze, 33–35

natural forms of pollution,
    10–11
nitric oxide, 10, 23, 24, 28
nitrogen, 10, 23
nitrogen dioxide, 23, 24, 27, 28
nitrogen oxide, 10, 20
North Pole, 9, 49
nuclear energy, 58

oxygen, 10, 23, 24, 28
ozone, 23–24, 27, 28, 36–37, 44,
    46, 49
ozone layer, 6, 8, 24, 45, 46–49

people and air pollution, 7, 15,
    16, 18, 26–28, 59
plants and air pollution, 7, 24,
    28–29, 49, 52–53
polar regions, 9, 46–49, 50, 58
pollution-control efforts, 16, 18,
    27, 56–59
power plants, 7, 22, 28, 35
pressure. *See* high pressure
    systems
prevailing winds, 32
primary pollutants, 23

scrubbers, 16, 19
sea breeze, 27, 35–37

secondary pollutants, 23–24
Seneca, 14
settling, 12
smog, 15, 20, 27
smoke, 10, 13–16, 20
solar energy, 17, 59
soot, 20, 31
Southern Hemisphere, 46–47
South Pole, 9, 46, 47–49
stable air conditions, 38–42
stagnation, 41
stratosphere, 8, 47, 49
stratospheric clouds, 47–48
sulfur, 18–19, 20, 24
sulfur dioxide, 10, 24, 28, 31,
    56–57
sulfuric acid, 24
Sun, 6, 8, 23, 39, 47, 49

temperature inversions, 40
thermosphere, 8
thunderstorms, 37–38
troposphere, 8

ultraviolet radiation, 8, 49
unstable air conditions, 37–38, 42

valley breeze, 33–35
Voiux, Harold Des, 15
volcanoes, 10, 11

water vapor, 23, 24, 43, 48
weather stations, 50, 55
wet deposition, 12, 25, 29, 31, 44
wind, 8, 9, 14, 16, 22, 32–42, 59
wind energy, 17

| METRIC CONVERSION CHART | | |
| --- | --- | --- |
| **When you know:** | **multiply by:** | **to find:** |
| acres | .41 | hectares |
| square miles | 2.59 | square kilometers |
| gallons | 3.79 | liters |
| inches | 2.54 | centimeters |
| feet | .30 | meters |
| yards | .91 | meters |
| miles | 1.61 | kilometers |
| pounds | .45 | kilograms |
| tons | .91 | metric tons |
| degrees Fahrenheit | .56 (after subtracting 32) | degrees Celsius |

# ACKNOWLEDGMENTS

Photographs and illustrations used with permission of: Visuals Unlimited (© Science VU), pp. 2, 11 [bottom], 19 [both], 25, 30 [top], (© J. Michael Eichelberger), p. 11 [top], (© Ken Lucas), p. 17 [top], (© Guillermo Gonzalez), p. 17 [bottom], (© John D. Cunningham), pp. 29, 37, (© A. J. Cunningham), p. 30 [bottom], (© Kjell B. Sandved), p. 33, (© Joe McDonald), pp. 43, 57, (© R. T. Domingo), p. 52, (© Albert Copley), p. 58, (© G. Prance), p. 61; © Thomas R. Fletcher, p. 7; Liz Monson, pp. 8, 34 [both], 36 [both], 39, 40, 51; © Betty Crowell, pp. 9, 21, 54; © Frank S. Balthis, pp. 12, 42, 47; Archive Photos, p. 14; CIDA/Roger Lemoyne, p. 18; Eda Rogers, pp. 27, 45 [bottom]; © Harry M. Walker Photography, p. 41; © Jo-Ann Ordano, p. 45 [top]; © Tom Pantages, p. 48.

Front cover: © Frank S. Balthis